The Supervisor's Guide to Federal Labor Relations

By

Dennis K. Reischl

and

Ralph R. Smith

Federal Personnel Management Institute, Inc.
3322 South Memorial Parkway
Suite 40
Huntsville, AL 35801

(205) 882-3042

ISBN 0-936295-08-2

Cover design by Beck Caneer, Madison, Alabama

Table of Contents

A Note of Thanks

Chapter One

Essential Information

Chapter Two

Making Changes

Chapter Three

Meetings With Employees

Chapter Four

Managing Under A Labor Agreement

Chapter Five

Handling Grievances

Chapter Six

Unfair Labor Practices

A Note of Thanks......

The Federal Personnel Management Institute, Inc. gratefully acknowledges the time and effort spent by the following people in reviewing and commenting on *The Supervisor's Guide to Federal Labor Relations*:

• James Alward, Labor Relations Specialist, Department of the Army, Washington, D.C.

• John Green, Labor Relations Specialist, Defense Logistics Agency, Alexandria, VA

• M. Lou Guest, Senior Labor Relations Advisor, Department of the Navy, Arlington, VA.

INTRODUCTION

As a supervisor or manager you have a lot of responsibility and probably operate under a lot of pressure. If you are like most busy managers, you want to focus as much of your time and attention as possible on simply getting your job done. And you want to spend as little time as possible on subjects that are not directly tied to accomplishing the mission—things like labor-management relations, for example.

Although that view is easy to understand, it misses an important point: Labor-relations activity is not an *extra* duty or requirement *outside* your main or real job, but a *direct part* of how you get your work done through employees—some of whom may be represented by a union. And if you are not able to recognize how and when labor relations issues come up in dealing with such represented employees, there is an excellent chance that the productivity of your work unit will suffer. Here are some examples:

> • A manager reassigns some duties from one position to another to improve work flow in his branch. The union then files something called an "unfair labor practice charge," and subsequently, a lot of time is spent discussing the matter with an investigator from the Federal Labor Relations Authority and agency labor relations specialists. Finally the supervisor is directed to return to the way things were done before.

• A new supervisor notices that an excessive amount of time is being used for breaks, but is told by employees that the breaks are a "past practice" and cannot be changed. Not sure what to do, she leaves things as they are.

• An employee demands a union representative before discussing his performance rating with his supervisor. The supervisor decides not to meet with the employee at all, and a grievance is filed.

• A manager directs several employees to work weekend overtime. Later, after the work is completed, other employees file a grievance claiming they were entitled to perform the work under the terms of the labor agreement. An arbitrator agrees and awards back pay, putting a dent in a budget that is already strained.

• While interviewing candidates for a vacancy in her shop a manager asks a union official how much official time he uses in performing representational duties. When the official is not selected, he files an unfair labor practice charge and is subsequently awarded a retroactive promotion and back pay.

There are several notable similarities in these examples. First, every one of them involves a typical, every-day decision made by an operating manager in the course of getting the job done—things like rearranging work flow, supervising the use of work time, rating performance, assigning overtime, and filling a vacant position.

Second, each of the examples involves, in one way or another, special rules that apply to managing unionized employees. Some of these rules are in the Federal Service Labor Relations Statute, while others are in a labor agreement.

Third, in each situation the failure of the manager to know or apply labor relations rules correctly and confidently has resulted in a problem that can cost the manager at least one of the three things he or she can least afford to waste: time, money, and the good will of the employees supervised.

Fourth, every one of these situations could be avoided or effectively handled by recognizing *when* labor relations responsibilities arise, *what rules* govern the situation, and *what options* are available to the manager.

The remainder of this book will give you the information you need to deal effectively with the situations outlined above, and with hundreds of others that come up every day throughout the Government.

Chapter One

Essential Information

INTRODUCTION

If you are like most managers and supervisors, the Federal labor-management relations program is something of a mystery. Lots of terms float around—such as grievance, ULP, arbitration, FLRA, management rights, official time, Weingarten meetings, bargaining, formal discussions, and the like—but often their meaning and, more importantly, how they apply to you, may be unclear.

The purpose of this chapter is to clear up the confusion by giving you a basic outline of how the Federal labor relations program is structured and operates. It will provide general information on the basic rights and responsibilities of agency management and unions, the outside agencies and parties that may become involved in labor relations issues, and where you fit in the process. Later chapters will provide more specific information and additional details on your role in dealing with particular labor relations matters.

BASIC RIGHTS UNDER THE LAW

The Federal Service Labor-Management Relations Statute (referred to as the law or the labor relations law throughout this book) is built on a number of specific rights that are granted to agency employees, unions, and agency management.

Employees' Rights

The most fundamental rights are those granted to employees. The law gives employees the right to organize themselves into a group—called a *bargaining unit*—and to select or create a particular *union* to represent the group in dealing with agency management. Employees are entitled to make efforts to form a bargaining unit and a union to represent the unit without interference, coercion, threats or retaliation from agency management. In short, the agency cannot try to influence employees in deciding whether to be represented by a union.

Furthermore, if a union is established, employees are free to join and assist the union if they choose to do so. Regardless of whether they join and pay dues to the union, employees included in a bargaining unit are entitled to receive representation and assistance from the union in dealing with agency management. The union's obligation to represent all employees regardless of whether they join the union or pay dues, is called the *duty of fair representation.*

Union Rights

Once a union has been selected to represent a bargaining unit of employees—usually through a secret ballot election—it gains several important rights. It is entitled to bargain with agency management over the personnel policies, practices and working conditions of bargaining unit employees. This means it is free to work out agreements about such things with agency management in labor contracts, and that it may also negotiate with the agency when management actions impact on the working conditions of bargaining unit employees.

The union also gains the right to represent bargaining unit employees in dealing with agency supervisors and managers in other situations. For example, the union is entitled to represent employees in grievances and investigatory discussions that could lead to discipline, and to attend certain meetings at which managers discuss the working conditions of unit employees.

Management Rights

The law also provides a substantial list of rights for agency management. In general, they can be broken down into three main categories. These are:

★ operational decisions

★ assignment of work

★ personnel actions.

Operational Decisions

In the area of operational decisions, the labor relations law gives management the right to decide its mission and determine how it will use its financial resources (budget); the organization and structure of an agency; the number, types and grades of employees it will employ to perform its work; the internal security practices that will be used to protect employees and equipment; what work, if any, will be contracted-out; and the particular methods, means and equipment (technology) it will use to accomplish its work.

Work Assignment

In assigning work to employees, the law gives management broad rights to determine what work will be done, when it will be performed and by which particular employees, and the qualifications necessary to perform the work.

Personnel Decisions

Finally, the law gives agency management the right to decide upon and carry out a broad range of personnel actions, such as hiring employees, promoting, rewarding, assigning, detailing, disciplining and detailing them, and even laying them off or removing them, if necessary.

HOW IT ALL WORKS

It is the expressed intent of the law that employees, unions and agency management will exercise their rights in such a way as to promote the effective and efficient operation of the agency. Here's how these rights are generally applied.

The agency—and its various components—makes basic decisions on what work will be done, how it will be done, how budgets will be spent, how many employees will be used to perform the work, and how the agency should be organized for maximum efficiency. In short, it makes the fundamental operating decisions on how the agency should be run.

On the other hand, the union, as the elected representative of a particular group of employees, usually negotiates a labor contract with agency management that establishes the personnel policies and working conditions of represented employees. Such contracts may cover a broad variety of subjects. For example, contracts often establish how promotions, discipline, reassignments and other personnel actions will be handled. They may also establish procedures for such things as leave scheduling, assignment to shifts and overtime scheduling. And they may also provide other rights and benefits, such as a temporary promotion and pay increase for assignment to a higher level job, parking preference, flexible work hours, and perhaps even child care arrangements for unit employees.

Finally, labor agreements always include a grievance and arbitration provision. If an employee, the union—or even management—believe that the labor agreement or a law, rule or regulation is not being followed properly, a grievance can be filed. And, if the problem cannot be worked out satisfactorily, either the union or agency management can call in an outside, temporary judge—called an *arbitrator*—to give a binding decision.

Operational Decisions

In carrying out their jobs and trying to operate as efficiently as possible, agency managers and supervisors often make operational decisions that affect employees. For example, a manager might decide to reorganize a branch, to change a particular work procedure, or to use a different method or piece of equipment to do a job. These decisions all fall within management's rights to operate the agency.

If the decisions affect the working conditions of represented employees, the union has the right to propose ways to reduce the impact on employees. The agency, in turn, must bargain on such union proposals. For example, in responding to the establishment of a new shift, a union might propose that assignments to the shift be made by first seeking volunteers, and then by assigning employees in order of seniority. In most cases, the negotiations process must be completed before implementing a decision or change that affects working conditions.

Day-to-Day Events

A variety of other matters come up in the normal course of business that also bring the basic rights of union and management into play. For example, if a supervisor suspected an employee had broken an important rule—such as smoking in a fuel storage area—management would have the right to investigate the matter and, if appropriate, to discipline the employee. The union, on the other hand, would have the right to represent the employee during the investigation of the matter, and also to provide representation if a grievance were filed. If the matter could not be worked out, the union would also have the right to take the dispute before an arbitrator under the provisions of the labor agreement.

On a more routine basis, management—through its supervisors and managers—makes a large number of decisions every day under rules established in the negotiated labor agreement. For example, supervisors make overtime assignments in accordance with established contract procedures; managers make promotion selections under agreed-upon merit promotion provisions; and supervisors grant annual leave and require some employees to produce doctor's slips to support sick leave requests under leave rules set up in the contract. Each of these decisions involves the exercise of both management and union rights under the law or the labor agreement.

WHO'S WHO

Two important questions have not yet been resolved. Which employees can be included in a bargaining unit, and which employees are part of agency management? Actually, as you will shortly see, these questions are simply different sides of the same coin.

Bargaining Unit Eligibility

The law provides that only certain categories of employees are eligible to be included in a bargaining unit and represented by a union. Supervisors, managers, personnel specialists, internal security personnel and confidential employees *cannot* be included in any bargaining unit. That may raise in your mind the reasonable question of "Which employees fit these descriptions?" Fortunately, the law provides reasonably clear answers.

Are You a Supervisor?

According to the law, you are a supervisor if you have the authority to take, or to effectively recommend taking, any *one* of the following actions for at least *one employee*:

☞Hire

☞Layoff

☞Suspend

☞Direct

☞Promote

☞Discipline

☞Transfer

☞Adjust grievances

☞ Recall

☞ Remove

☞ Furlough

☞ Reward

☞ Assign

Are You a Manager?

Most managers are also supervisors, and are easily identified as representatives of agency management on that basis. But the law recognizes that there will some employees who do not actually supervise anyone, but who are still a member of the management team. These people are called *management officials*. For example, a person who serves as the Executive Director of an agency, but who does not directly supervise any employees, would normally be considered a "management official" and, therefore, a representative of agency management when dealing with a union or bargaining unit employee. Employees are designated as "management officials" if they make or influence the development of agency policy.

Why Is It Important to Identify Managers and Supervisors?

It is important to be able to identify managers and supervisors because, as representatives of agency management, their actions are usually binding on the agency. Therefore, supervisors and managers have the power to reach agreement with union representatives, to make decisions on grievances filed by employees and unions, and to commit violations of the labor contract or the labor relations statute for which the agency is held accountable.

Supervisors have authority to:

★ Reach agreements with a union

★ Make decisions on grievances

★ Violate the contract or labor relations statute

Other Excluded Employees

Confidential employees are those whose duties routinely expose them to confidential labor relations information used by the agency. For example, the secretary to the agency's labor relations officer, or a secretary to the personnel officer of the agency are normally considered to be confidential employees, and therefore are excluded from the bargaining unit.

Employees engaged in Federal personnel work are those in the various personnel specialties, such as staffing, classification or employee relations positions, who are performing other than purely clerical duties.

Investigative employees directly involved in the agency's internal security include employees performing internal auditing functions, such as an Inspector General's office, or an internal security office.

Why Is This Important To You?

In dealing with labor relations issues, the first thing you need to know is whether an employee is part of a bargaining unit. If an employee is not in a bargaining unit, the employee is not represented by a union, and none of the provisions of any labor agreement apply to that person. On the other hand, if an employee is in a unit, both the provisions of the law and a labor agreement apply. While you do not need a program to know who the players are, you do need to know which team they are on to do your job properly.

Where To Look

To find out whether an employee is included in a bargaining unit, look at the bargaining unit description that is normally included in the first or second article of a labor agreement. It will tell you which categories of employees are included in and excluded from the bargaining unit. *If the unit description is not included in your agreement or if you are still not sure whether an employee is covered, contact your agency's labor relations office for help.*

Role Of The Labor Relations Office

The labor relations specialists in your agency are there to help you manage your organization effectively by providing expert, up-to-date advice. If you have any questions about how to handle a problem, call them for advice. They are there to help you and you will find them more than willing to do so. By asking questions and seeking advice in advance, you will make your job easier and you will get more valuable help from the labor relations office as well. It is usually much easier to avoid or correct a problem when it first starts than it is to straighten things out later.

OUTSIDE ACTORS

Occasionally organizations other than agency management and the union also get involved in the agency's labor relations issues. One situation already mentioned is when the union and management call in an outside arbitrator for grievance decisions. Other outside parties may also get involved.

These outside parties and the situations in which they become involved are outlined below.

Federal Labor Relations Authority

If an employee, the union or management think that the Federal Service Labor-Management Relations Statute has been violated in some way, an unfair labor practice (ULP) charge can be filed. For example, if a union believed that you had made a change affecting the working conditions of bargaining unit employees without allowing the union to bargain, it could file a charge with an organization called the Federal Labor Relations Authority (FLRA or Authority). The FLRA would investigate the matter, attempt to settle the problem, and if necessary, hold a hearing and give a final decision on the issue. More detailed information on unfair labor practices, how they are handled and how they affect you is contained in Chapter Six.

Federal Service Impasses Panel

Similarly, if management and the union cannot agree and subsequently reach a deadlock in bargaining, either on a labor contract or about the impact of an operational change affecting unit employees, either side can ask for the help of an organization called the Federal Service Impasses Panel (FSIP or the Panel). As a first step the Panel usually requires the parties to try to reach agreement voluntarily with the help of a mediator from the Federal Mediation and Conciliation Service (FMCS). But if they are still unable to work out their differences, the Panel will listen to each side's position and issue a decision on what agreement provisions the parties must adopt. A more detailed summary of when and how you may become involved in bargaining over operational changes is contained in Chapter Two.

As you can see, outside parties normally become involved only when invited in by either management or the union—or both. They exist to provide labor-management relations assistance to the parties in dealing with problem situations of one sort or another. But in the majority of cases, it is possible—and always preferable—to work out problems and issues in-house. As a general rule, it is better to call for such outside assistance only when it is really necessary.

ROLE OF THE MANAGER AND SUPERVISOR

As you may have noticed in reading this chapter, supervisors and managers are directly involved in dealing with management, union and employee rights under the law. It is easy to see why. You make the day-to-day decisions that involve laws, rules, regulations and negotiated rules; you communicate directly with employees on a wide range of matters; and you handle the problems and complaints that crop up over whether existing rules are being properly applied. You are also often involved in making changes and improvements in operational methods that may impact on employees' working conditions. That is why it is essential that you understand how to recognize and deal with labor relations situations effectively.

Key Points

1. The Federal labor relations law establishes basic rights for employees, unions and agency management. Employees have the right to form, join and assist a union. Unions have the right to bargain on behalf of employees and to represent them in dealings with management. Management has the right to operate the agency, to assign work and to make basic personnel decisions.

2. A group of employees who choose to be represented by a union is called a bargaining unit. The union selected to represent the unit must represent the interests of all employees in the bargaining unit.

3. Supervisors, managers, personnel specialists, confidential employees and internal security employees are not eligible to be included in any bargaining unit.

4. An employee is a supervisor if he or she has authority to take or effectively recommend personnel actions affecting one or more employees.

5. An employee is a management official if he or she has the authority to make or effectively influence the development of agency policy.

6. All supervisors or managers represent agency management in dealing with employees or unions, and have the authority under the labor relations statute to take actions that are binding on an agency.

7. Once established, a union has the right to bargain with agency management over the personnel policies, practices and working conditions of bargaining unit employees.

8. When management makes operational decisions that affect the working conditions of bargaining unit employees, the union has the right to propose and bargain on ways to reduce the impact of management's action on unit employees.

9. In making numerous day-to-day decisions, such as assigning work and dealing with employee problems and requests, operating managers and supervisors are involved in applying management and union rights under the law and labor contracts.

10. Outside actors, including arbitrators, the FLRA, FMCS and the FSIP become involved in dealing with labor relations issues when invited in by either party. Their function is to help resolve special problems.

11. Your agency's labor relations specialists are available to provide expert advice and assistance, and should be contacted for help whenever necessary.

Chapter Two

Making Changes

INTRODUCTION

What kind of changes have occurred in your agency, and in your particular organization over the past several years? If you think about it, chances are that you will be able to identify quite a few. Your part of the agency may have added or reduced employees, changed the way work is assigned or carried out, adopted new or different equipment, changed or improved operating methods, relocated to new space, changed rules on smoking, added a new shift, or adopted a flextime arrangement. Change is inevitable, because organizations—like people—must constantly adjust to things going on around them if they are to succeed and survive in an ever-changing world.

But why is this important in thinking about labor-management relations and your part in it? For at least three good reasons.

> ★ First, because many, if not most changes of the kind listed above affect the working conditions of bargaining unit employees, and therefore bring into play the union's right to bargain with agency management.

> ★ Second, because the failure to recognize the union's right to become involved when changes occur produces over three-fourths of all unfair labor practice (ULP) disputes in the Federal service every year.

★ And third, because if you are able to understand and recognize when changes in your operation bring the union's rights into the picture, you will be able to avoid one of the biggest causes of time-wasting, expensive disputes that plague operating managers.

In short, by understanding this one key part of the law, you will be able to save time, make changes and improvements more quickly and smoothly, and avoid the headache and expense of unnecessary disputes with your union. This chapter will explain how to recognize when you need to involve the union in making the changes.

CONDITIONS OF EMPLOYMENT

Your decision to make a change will bring into play the union's right to become involved only if the change involves the *conditions of employment* of bargaining unit employees. It is important to understand what is meant by this term.

Bargaining unit employees' conditions of employment include two general areas: *personnel policies and practices*, and other *working conditions*. Neither category is difficult to understand.

Personnel Policies & Practices

In general, the rules and procedures that prescribe how employees behave or how they will be managed—such as leave policies, dress codes, merit promotion policies, discipline procedures and the like—are called *personnel policies and practices.* These rules and procedures apply to *people*—employees—and therefore are called *personnel* policies and practices.

As a rule of thumb, *written rules* for managing employees, such as an annual leave scheduling procedure or merit promotion rules, may be considered *policies. Unwritten rules* related to employees, such as an established pattern of allowing employees to swap weekend overtime assignments, are usually called *practices.* An established pattern of doing things one particular way may become an unwritten rule—a *past practice*—if it is followed consistently, for a long period of time, with the knowledge and acceptance of both the union and management. These patterns may become a binding condition of employment if they do not conflict with any law, regulation, contract provision or management right.

Working Conditions

Other miscellaneous features and benefits of employees' work environment—such as heat, light, air conditioning, parking arrangements, safety conditions, availability of food, and the like—fall under the general heading of *working conditions.*

Taken together, these two categories of personnel *policies and practices* and *working conditions* make up the *conditions of employment* of bargaining unit employees.

The most important thing to recognize is that a management decision or action that changes employees' conditions of employment brings the union's rights into the picture, and requires you to do certain things. Your responsibilities in these situations will be explained later in this chapter. First, however, it is essential that you understand how to spot situations that involve changes in conditions of employment. Managers and supervisors usually become involved in them in one of the two ways explained below.

OPERATIONAL CHANGES

If you were to look closely at the list of common changes mentioned above, you would notice that they could be divided into two general categories or kinds of changes. The first could be called *operational* or *work-related* changes. These would include changes in such things as the equipment used to perform work, the number of employees assigned to a shift or task, the way the organization is structured, or the work procedures used. These changes are called *operational changes* because they are directed at how *the work* is to be accomplished.

As a general rule, operational changes fall within agency management's protected rights under the law. For example, the labor relations law grants management the right to determine how to organize its employees; to determine what technology or equipment will be used to accomplish the work; to decide how many employees are necessary on a particular shift or project to complete the work; to decide which duties a particular position or occupation should perform; and to decide what particular methods will be used to carry out the work.

As a result, you and the other managers in your agency have the right to decide upon and carry out changes in the way such things are done when you determine they are appropriate to improve the effectiveness and efficiency of the operation. And the basic decision to make such changes is not open to negotiation with a union. **Nevertheless, if such an operational change produces an impact on the working conditions of unit employees, the union is entitled to propose ways to deal with the impact—and you and other managers are required to bargain on these proposals.**

For example, if you or managers above you decided to reorganize and move your part of the organization to a different location in order to improve efficiency or cut costs, the decision to do so would be completely up to management. The decision to reorganize would not be open to negotiation because it is covered by the protected management right to determine the appropriate organizational structure. But if the reorganization/relocation changed employees' working conditions in any significant way, their union would have the right to become involved by making proposals to deal with the changes.

In this example, such proposals might include proposals on how to arrange smoking and non-smoking areas, procedures for assigning work space, requests for snack vending machines, and ways of assigning parking spaces. Again, the basic decision to reorganize and relocate would be completely up to management, but the union would have the right to become involved in working out how the decision would affect the work lives of employees.

Working out such procedures and arrangements for dealing with the effect a protected management decision has upon employees is usually called *impact and implementation bargaining*. It affects operating managers more often than any other union right. Later in this chapter you will learn how to recognize such situations and what to do when you spot them.

OTHER CHANGES

Not all changes in an organization involve how the work is to be accomplished, however. Some changes involve rules on how employees are required to conduct themselves or how they are to be managed in the workplace. For example, the adoption of new smoking rules or a new dress code would not involve how the *work* is done or what equipment will be used to do it, but rather, how *employees* will act in the workplace. Similarly, a decision to eliminate rest periods or to no longer allow coffee to be brewed in an office area would not directly involve operational decisions on what work will be done, or when or how it will be accomplished. Rather, they would establish or change rules for employee behavior in the workplace. Because decisions on such matters are not covered by any specific, protected management right, *the decision itself* is open to negotiation.

To continue the example, if you or a higher level manager decided that a stricter dress code should be put in place or that coffee should no longer be allowed in the work area, the proposed new rule would be completely open to negotiation with the union, because neither decision involves a protected management right. In such cases the *substance* of the change is negotiable.

Management Rights

● **The agency's mission, budget and organization**

● **Numbers, types and grades of employees**

● **Technology, equipment and methods of performing work**

● **Assignment of work and contracting out of work**

● **Decisions to hire, fire, layoff, reward, or promote employees**

● **Select employees from any appropriate source**

The Bottom Line

So the basic rule is this. If the change you want to make is covered by a protected management right, only the impact and implementation of the change is open to negotiation with the union. On the other hand, if the intended change is not covered by an absolute management right, the proposed change itself is open to bargaining.

Recognizing Your Obligations

But regardless of whether the impact or the substance of a change is bargainable, the key thing for you to recognize is that you are required by law to give the union a chance to negotiate if the intended change will significantly affect the personnel policies and practices or general working conditions of unit employees. The way to spot such situations is to ask yourself the following questions *before* putting a management decision into effect:

1. Will my decision produce a change, or will it simply use an existing rule or way of doing things?

For example, implementing a new way of offering overtime work to employees would be a change. Simply assigning employees to work overtime under the existing overtime assignment procedure would not be a change.

2. What employees will this decision affect?

If it will affect bargaining unit employees there may be an obligation to inform and deal with the union. If the decision only affects employees outside the bargaining unit, such as managers and supervisors, no union rights are involved.

3. Will the decision alter the working conditions or personnel policies and practices of unit employees?

If not, there is no obligation to bargain. For example, replacing old video terminals used in word processing with new equipment that operates the same way would not change employees working conditions or personnel policies in any way, and therefore would not involve the union's right to become involved.

4. Will the change significantly affect employees' working conditions, or is it trivial?

A change in the color of a standard form used to log mileage is unlikely to have any significant impact on working conditions. On the other hand, changing shift starting times probably will have an important impact on employees. As a general rule, if you are not certain whether an intended change will produce significant impact, your best bet is either to obtain the advice of your labor relations specialist or simply to assume there is significant impact.

If you are able to answer 'yes' or 'probably' to all four of the questions outlined above, the union that represents bargaining unit employees has the right to become involved in dealing with your intended change. If so, it is your legal responsibility to provide them the opportunity to bargain on the change. Here's how you do it.

LIKE A PING-PONG GAME

Step One - The Serve

When you decide to make a change and determine that the change will bring into play the union's right to deal with the issue, you set in motion a series of steps that operate a lot like a ping-pong or tennis game. The first thing the law requires you to do is to notify the union of the intended change *before* you put it into effect. That puts the ball in the union's court. If you are not sure of the proper union official to notify, contact your labor relations advisor for assistance.

Before looking at the next stage of the game, it is important to note several things about this requirement to notify the union. First, the notification must be made to the *union* first, not to employees first or to everyone at the same time. Second, the union should be notified of *what* you intend to do and *when* you plan to put it into effect, and the notification must be made *reasonably in advance* of the intended change.

How much advance notice is "reasonable" will depend on the importance and complexity of the change. A new requirement that employees in an office stagger their lunch periods to provide telephone coverage probably requires no more than a week or two advance notice. An extensive reorganization and relocation of employees would require considerably more notice, perhaps a month or more.

In either event, the important thing is to avoid last minute notification or, worse yet, making the change without notification at all. Such situations produce the vast majority of all unfair labor practice charges, and create time-consuming disputes that adversely affect labor-management relations.

In some cases labor agreements provide for a specific number of days notice of a change. To find out whether your labor agreement has such a provision, review the sections dealing with impact bargaining or contact your labor relations advisor for assistance.

The Next Step

Meanwhile, back to the ping-pong game. Assume that you have gotten an idea for a change that will improve the efficiency of your part of the organization, thought it over and determined that the union should be notified. So you provide the union reasonable advance notice of what will happen and when. Now what?

Basically, one of two things. Either you will receive no response to your announcement of an intended change—in which case you can simply put the change into effect as of the date you indicated—or the union will request to bargain. Actually, the union may respond in any of several ways. It may request to meet; it may send proposals to you; it may request additional information about the intended change; or it may request a delay in carrying out the change to allow it more time to develop its position. Any of these responses are adequate to indicate its intention to bargain with the agency concerning the change. In effect, any such response puts the ball back into your court.

Back In Your Court

If the ball lands back in your court, the law's requirement to "bargain in good faith" will require you or your agency's labor relations specialists to take whatever steps are appropriate. For example, if the union has requested relevant and available information related to the change, you will have to provide it. If the union asks to meet to discuss the change and to get a clearer picture of what you intend to do, you are obliged to do so. And if the union puts forth proposals for dealing with the change, you must bargain on them insofar as they are negotiable. That is, insofar as they relate to the change and do not violate law, controlling regulations or management rights under the Federal labor relations statute.

In most cases, should the union respond to an intended change by requesting bargaining, your best bet is to contact your agency's labor relations specialists for advice and assistance. They will be up to date on what is and is not negotiable, and they will know how to proceed from this point on.

In the overwhelming majority of situations, managers and local union officials are able to work out mutually satisfactory arrangements to deal with such changes with few problems. In some situations, however, you may not be able to reach agreement, and professional advice and assistance will be necessary in dealing with the resulting deadlock—or *impasse* as it is called in labor relations terminology.

COMMON MISTAKES

Unfortunately, dealing with changes leads to more conflict and problems than any other situation in Federal labor-management relations. Here are the most common mistakes managers make in this area.

★ Failure to notify the union reasonably in advance of a change that affects unit employees' working conditions.

★ Refusing to provide information related to an intended change that is relevant, necessary and reasonably available.

★ Mistakenly refusing to bargain because an intended change involves a management right. Even so, the *impact* of the change on employees' working conditions is often negotiable.

★ Trying to slip changes past the union in order to avoid bargaining. Often such attempts result in ULP charges and, ultimately, a return to square one.

PRACTICAL ADVICE

A few practical points—most of them common sense—will help you meet your responsibilities under this part of the law.

First and most important is this. Be alert to situations that will bring the union's rights into the picture. The key is change. Whenever you are about to make a change, first ask yourself the four questions outlined earlier in this chapter. If you do you will wind up saving yourself a lot of time and headaches later.

How to Recognize Your Bargaining Obligations

★ Will the decision change the way something is done?

★ What employees will be affected?

★ Will the decision change conditions of employment of unit members?

★ Is the change significant?

Second, err on the side of *more* communication with union officials rather than less. In other words, if you're not sure whether you are really required to notify or talk with the union about a matter, it's generally safer—and smarter—to communicate. It also may help you to build a better working relationship with your union counterpart.

Third, when a change does impact on employees' working conditions and the union seeks to bargain about it, take a problem-solving approach to the issue. Trying to "win" the resulting negotiations usually just leads to frustration and often to completely avoidable conflicts and hard feelings. The point is to get the mission accomplished in an effective and efficient manner, not to score points in dealing with the union.

Finally, use your labor relations professionals for advice and assistance. After all, that's what they are paid for. Some issues can become complicated, and new decisions and approaches are constantly arriving on the scene in Federal labor-management relations. So if you have any doubt at all about how to handle a situation, contact your agency's labor relations specialists for help. If they do not have the answers you need right at hand, they can usually find them very quickly.

Your objective is to get your mission accomplished—not to score points in dealing with the union.

Key Points

1. While most changes made by managers are operational or work related, some involve personnel rules and practices that apply to employees.

2. If an operational or personnel management decision results in a change or impact upon the conditions of employment for bargaining unit employees, their union is entitled to become involved and to bargain with management about the change.

3. Most operational changes involve the use of protected management rights. In these situations only proposals on the *impact and implementation* of the change are open to negotiation.

4. Changes that are not based on a protected management right, which often include changes to personnel policies and practices, are completely open to negotiation.

5. If an intended change will affect unit employees' working conditions or the personnel policies and practices that apply to them, management is required to provide reasonable advance notice to the union *before* the change is put into effect.

6. Upon being notified of an intended change, the union is entitled to request relevant, necessary and available information related to the change and to make proposals related to the change.

7. Your agency's labor relations practitioners are an essential source of advice and assistance in dealing with change situations.

Chapter Three

Meetings with Employees

INTRODUCTION

As a supervisor or manager you are probably in constant communication with bargaining unit employees on a wide range of subjects. Stop and think for a moment about the various things you talk with employees about. More than likely, you will quickly develop a list of conversations you often have over matters such as work assignments and direction, performance evaluation and counseling, gripes and suggestions from employees, and discussions of topics unrelated to work like the weather or sports.

In the majority of situations, you have no obligation to involve union representatives in such direct discussions with unit employees. But the law sets up two specific situations in which the union does have the right to become involved in your discussions with bargaining unit employees. It is important that you be able to recognize these two situations and effectively deal with them. They are called *formal discussions* and *investigative* or *Weingarten meetings*.

FORMAL DISCUSSIONS

The concept of *formal discussions* is easiest to understand if you keep in mind the central role and function of the union. As we pointed out in Chapter One, when employees select a union to represent them as a group, the union becomes the "exclusive representative" of that group—which is known as the *bargaining unit*. The primary purpose of the union is to represent employees in establishing and changing *conditions of employment.* That is, in the establishment or change of the personnel policies, practices and overall working conditions that apply to bargaining unit employees. In short, you might think of unit employees' conditions of employment as being within the turf or charter of the union. Consequently, as we pointed out in Chapter Two, any changes in such conditions of employment must be negotiated with the union, not directly with employees.

In recognition of this fact, the law takes an additional step. It provides that when a **management representative**, such as a manager, supervisor or personnel specialist, wants to have a **substantive discussion** with one or more **bargaining unit employees** about **conditions of employment or a grievance**, the union must be notified and given a chance to attend the discussion. The idea behind this requirement is really quite simple. Since the union is responsible for working out and enforcing the conditions of employment with management, it should be allowed to sit in when managers discuss such matters with the employees represented by the union.

Your first task is to learn how to recognize such situations when they arise so that you can meet the requirements of the law. The following rules of thumb will help you over this first hurdle.

Recognizing Formal Discussions

The best way to spot formal discussions is by asking yourself a few simple questions if you are about to get involved in a meeting with employees.

1. Who will attend the meeting?

Will the meeting/discussion involve both a person who represents management (for example, a manager, supervisor, or personnel specialist) and at least one employee who is in the bargaining unit? If not, no formal discussion is possible. If the answer is yes, however, there remains a possibility it may be a formal discussion. If so, go on to the next question.

2. What will be discussed at the meeting?

Will the discussion involve either a give-and-take conversation about, or a detailed, one-sided explanation of a personnel policy or practice or general working condition that applies to unit employees? For example, will it concern how weekend overtime should be assigned or whether employees should be allowed to smoke in a break room? If so, it is probably a formal discussion. If, on the other hand, the discussion will focus only on work-related matters, such as how to operate equipment or which assignments must be completed by a particular date, the meeting will not be a formal discussion.

Similarly, will the meeting involve the discussion of a grievance filed under the negotiated labor agreement, an appeal filed as a result of a disciplinary action against an employee or an Equal Employment Opportunity (EEO) complaint? If so, the meeting may be considered a formal discussion by the Federal Labor Relations Authority (FLRA) because of the impact that a management decision could have on general conditions of employment for unit employees.

Therefore, if a meeting might require a discussion of either general conditions of employment or an active grievance or appeal, a third question must be asked.

3. Is the meeting/discussion "formal" or simply a casual conversation?

This provision of the law is not intended to require the presence of a union representative every time some aspect of working conditions or a personnel policy is mentioned in passing. Rather, it is intended to cover serious, substantive discussions of matters within the union's turf. To determine whether a discussion is casual or trivial rather than serious, the FLRA looks at how "formal" the meeting is. If it is pre-scheduled, attended by several persons on either side, has a definite agenda, is recorded in formal notes or minutes, or if employees are required to attend, it is more likely to be seen as a formal discussion.

On the other hand, if a meeting just consists of some gripes or suggestions discussed in passing, or a question about when a grievance decision will be rendered, the discussion will not be viewed as a formal meeting.

The Next Step

If the answer to all three questions is 'yes,' the agency is required to inform a representative of the union *before* holding the meeting or discussion so that the union can arrange to have a representative attend the meeting if it chooses. Depending on the size and location of the meeting, as well as the wording of your labor agreement, agency management might inform any union official from the president on down to the steward of a particular work group. Once you have done so, it is up to the union to decide whether it wishes to have a representative attend the meeting. If it is not informed of the meeting and does not have a representative in attendance, the union's right to be given the opportunity to attend such meetings will have been violated, and an unfair labor practice will have been committed.

> **NOTE: Whether the employee wants the union to be present at the meeting is not important. The right to attend such meetings is a right given to the union by the statute. It is not a right that may be given away by individual employees.**

Helpful Hints

To get a handle on how and when formal discussions come up, it will help to think about what kinds of meetings and discussions are *not* formal discussions. These include:

> • Discussions solely between management officials and supervisors;
>
> • Discussions between a supervisor and an employee who is not in the bargaining unit (for example, a personnel specialist or other supervisors);

• Discussions about work procedures, work assignments, deadlines, equipment and its use, or guidance on how to perform an assignment.

• Discussions concerning the establishment of performance standards, an employee's performance relative to established standards, or performance counseling.

• Discussions about an employee's conduct, counseling or warnings concerning conduct, or suggestions for improvement.

In short, very few meetings with employees are formal discussions that require notice to the union in advance.

Role of the Union Representative

If and when you do have a meeting that is a formal discussion and the union chooses to attend, what role, if any, is a union representative entitled to play in the meeting?

In general, a union representative is entitled to take an active role, but not to the extent of taking over or disrupting the meeting. Because a union representative is there as the official representative of unit employees, he or she has the right to ask questions related to the topics under discussion, to state the union's opinions or views on such matters, and to disagree with the points being made in the meeting by management officials. This does not include the right to disrupt the meeting, however, to bring it to a halt or to take it over. Moreover, although a representative may well disagree with management's point of view and express his or her disagreement, the representative is not entitled to engage in grossly disrespectful or antagonistic behavior.

A union representative is entitled to take any of these actions at a formal discussion:

★ Ask questions related to the matters under discussion at the meeting

★ Make relevant remarks concerning such matters

★ State the union's position on the matters under discussion

Formal Discussion Checklist

In order to decide if a meeting is a formal discussion, ask these questions:

I. Who is at the meeting?

> Is there a representative of management and a member of the bargaining unit?

II. What is the subject of the meeting?

> Is the subject of the meeting a grievance filed by a unit employee?
>
> Does the discussion concern a condition of employment?

III. Is the meeting formal?

> Is there an agenda?
>
> Are employees required to attend?
>
> Are notes or minutes kept?
>
> How many managers are present?

A meeting may be a formal discussion only if the meeting is between a member of management and a bargaining unit member, the subject is on a grievance or a condition of employment, and the meeting is formal in nature.

INVESTIGATIVE OR WEINGARTEN MEETINGS

The second special situation in which the Federal labor relations statute gives a union the right to represent employees in meetings with management is called an "examination in connection with an investigation." In plain English these conversations are usually referred to as *investigative* or *Weingarten meetings*.

Background

A little background will give you an idea of what such discussions are all about, and let you know how the name Weingarten got in the picture.

The name Weingarten, when used in connection with investigative meetings, springs from a private sector case decided by the U.S. Supreme Court in 1975. In that case, management had suspected an employee of minor theft, and had called her in to ask questions. The employee insisted on having a union representative present to help her respond to the questions. The company refused to allow such assistance, and when the employee refused to answer the questions without a representative present, she was ultimately fired. An unfair labor practice complaint was then filed and eventually made its way to the Supreme Court.

In its decision the Court determined that, in situations in which an employee is being questioned by a management representative and reasonably fears that disciplinary action may be taken, the employee is entitled to the help of a union representative if he or she asks for such assistance.

When the Federal Service Labor-Management Relations Statute was enacted some three years later, the same idea was written into the law. Based on the same factors that the Supreme Court outlined in the private sector case, the law establishes four requirements for a meeting to be considered an investigative meeting at which unit employees are entitled to union representation:

1. Attendance

The meeting must include *both* a management representative—such as a manager, supervisor, personnel specialist or security officer—*and* a bargaining unit employee.

2. Nature

The discussion must be *investigative* in nature. That is, questions are being asked of the employee. If the discussion is *not* investigative, it will not qualify. For example, routine work discussions or a performance evaluation do not involve an *investigation*, and therefore do not fit under this category.

3. Reasonable Fear

The employee must *"reasonably fear"* that discipline might result from the discussion. This means that, based on all the circumstances—including what the employee knows that you may not—if a reasonable person could fairly conclude that a meeting or discussion might result in discipline, this requirement will be met. Note that this requirement is based on the employee's perceptions, *not* whether you intend to discipline the employee at the time she asks for a representative.

4. Request for Representation

The employee must *request* assistance. Unlike the situation involving formal discussions, employees must request the help of a representative to be entitled to one.

The law *does not* require you to advise an employee of the right to representation before you ask questions. However, your labor agreement might add such a requirement, so read it carefully before questioning an employee.

The Bottom Line

If all four requirements are met, the meeting qualifies as an investigative or Weingarten meeting, and you are faced with several possible courses of action.

Options

The law gives you several options in dealing with situations like this when you are conducting a meeting:

> ★ You can stop the meeting and not call in a union representative.

★ You can temporarily stop the questioning long enough to obtain a union representative, and then continue the questioning after the union representative has arrived.

★ You can remove the employee's "reasonable fear" of discipline by stating that the employee will not be disciplined—in which case the employee is no longer entitled to the help of a representative. (This option should be exercised carefully. You may not know in what activities the employee has been involved and third party decisions do not always honor this "trust me" approach.)

So, for example, if you call an employee into your office and ask questions about whether the employee had altered a doctor's certificate, and the employee requests a union representative to be present, you would either have to allow a representative to attend the remainder of the discussion, or end the meeting, or assure the employee that there will be no discipline. If you do none of the above, but continue to question the employee without a representative present, you would be violating the law. In that case, any later discipline based on the employee's answers might be overturned.

Role of the Union Representative

As in formal discussions, if a union represents an employee in a Weingarten meeting, the representative is entitled to take an active role. This means that he or she may ask questions that are reasonably related to the matter being discussed, and may raise relevant questions that will help the employee tell his or her side of the story.

Remember, however, that it is still your meeting. The union representative does *not* have the right to answer your questions for the employee, to break up the meeting, or to try to prevent you from carrying out your investigation of the matter. You have the right to ask—and receive answers to—questions you have for the employee.

What's Not Covered

The Federal Labor Relations Authority has decided that employees have the right to have a union representative present only when the discussion could lead to *discipline*. (That is, to a reprimand, suspension or removal for misconduct.) Discussions concerning an employee's *performance*, even though such discussions could lead to a poor performance rating or to a performance-based action, do not bring the Weingarten right into play. Needless to say, other routine conversations that do not involve a reasonable fear of discipline are not covered under this right either.

Weingarten Meeting Checklist

● Is the meeting between a member of the bargaining unit and a management representative?

● Are questions being asked of the employee?

● Can the employee reasonably fear disciplinary action will result from the meeting?

● Has the employee requested representation by the union?

If all four criteria have been met, the meeting qualifies as a Weingarten meeting.

OTHER MEETINGS WITH MANAGEMENT

Some labor agreements provide that employees may be represented in other kinds of meetings also. For example, some agreements allow employees to have a union representative present at performance evaluation discussions. Check with your labor relations advisor and read your particular labor agreement if you are not sure whether the union has the right to represent employees in any other kinds of meetings.

Notice to Employees

The agency is required to advise all employees of their Weingarten right once each year. This is usually done through a general posting or a mailing to employees by your personnel or labor relations office. Generally, you are not required to advise the employee at the beginning of the meeting of the right to union representation. However, it is always a good idea to check the collective bargaining agreement to see if there are requirements above and beyond what is required by the labor relations statute.

Generally, you do not have to advise an employee of a right to representation at the beginning of a meeting. But check your labor agreement to see if you have any obligations beyond what is required by the statute.

Key Points

1. Union representatives have the right to represent bargaining unit employees in several kinds of meetings between management representatives and unit employees.

2. One type of such meetings, called a formal discussion, involves discussion of personnel policies, practices, general working conditions, or grievances that have been filed under the labor agreement. Agency management is required to notify the union of such meetings in advance and to give it a chance to have a representative attend.

3. Union representatives may also attend investigative meetings that may lead to discipline if an employee asks for representation. Such meetings are often referred to as Weingarten meetings.

4. In both kinds of meetings representatives are allowed to take an active role by raising relevant questions, making appropriate comments and presenting the union's viewpoint.

5. As a supervisor, you have the right to maintain control of such meetings by requiring the employee to answer questions rather than having the union answer.

Chapter Four

Managing Under
a Labor
Agreement

INTRODUCTION

The negotiation of a labor agreement is obviously an important event, and it draws a lot of attention for understandable reasons. But it is only a small part of agency management's labor relations responsibility. When the negotiations are over, the contract is still nothing more than words on paper. It will not be a useful, working document until operating supervisors and managers put it into effect in handling everyday issues in the workplace. And that is where you play a very important role in your agency's labor relations program.

THE SUPERVISOR'S ROLE IN CONTRACT ADMINISTRATION

Supervisors and managers are a primary ingredient for a successful labor relations program in any Federal agency. If you know what is in the contract and do a solid job of applying it in day-to-day work situations, the labor relationship is usually successful. But if supervisors and managers do not understand their role or do not handle it well, the efforts of all the lawyers, negotiators and labor relations specialists money can buy will be insufficient to create a productive, working relationship. A brief examination of the functions performed by supervisors and managers in contract administration will explain why.

Managers and Supervisors Administer the Contract

You may not have realized it, but many of the daily decisions you make in managing represented employees involve the interpretation and use of rules set up in the labor agreement. For example, if two employees want the same day off on annual leave but only one can be spared, the immediate supervisor will usually determine who has first choice. If the employees involved are in a bargaining unit covered by a labor agreement, it is up to the supervisor to find out what rule, if any, the contract sets up for handling such situations, and then to apply that rule in a fair, reasonable and consistent manner.

To provide another example, if the contract says that a union representative is entitled to a "reasonable" amount of official time, you would be responsible for determining how much time is "reasonable." If representatives are normally allowed no more than one hour to investigate a grievance, you may limit the use of official time to one hour. On the other hand, if the matter is unusually complicated, you might allow more time than usual.

Regardless of your decision, it is important to recognize that in making such a decision you are *interpreting* and *applying* the labor agreement. And you probably do so in hundreds of other situations without even thinking of it. For example, in assigning overtime, applying smoking rules, authorizing environmental differential pay, making a shift assignment, or doing any of the thousands of other routine tasks involved in managing employees, chances are that you are applying the terms of the labor agreement.

Managers and Supervisors Handle Contract Problems and Disputes

Your decisions will not always be accepted without question by employees and unions. This is particularly true where the union's interpretation of a contract provision may be different from yours. For example, if employees or their union felt that you had reached an incorrect decision on who should be directed to work a holiday overtime assignment, they could challenge your decision by filing a grievance.

Usually such grievances seek to overturn or change a supervisor's original decision and, depending on the issue at hand, sometimes seek a "remedy" or "relief." In the overtime situation, for example, the union might seek payment of overtime pay on behalf of grievants who believe they were improperly denied the overtime assignment under the contract.

Under most contract grievance procedures the supervisor or manager who made the disputed decision is given the first opportunity to change it. Then, if the union or grieving employee is not satisfied with that official's response to the grievance, the matter can usually be appealed to higher levels of management as outlined in the grievance procedure.

As a result, managers may become involved in interpreting and applying a contract either at the initial decision level, or in reviewing the actions and decisions of subordinate managers.

Supervisors May Be Called to Testify in Arbitration Hearings

Ultimately, if a dispute between the union and management is not settled, the problem may be placed before an outside arbitrator who will determine how the contract should be interpreted and applied.

To help in reaching a decision, arbitrators usually hold an informal hearing to gather facts. The facts presented at hearing may be documents, correspondence, testimony or even demonstrations and site tours.

At these hearings the agency's presentation is usually built on the direct testimony of managers and supervisors. On occasion the union may also call a manager or supervisor as a witness if it has questions it wants to ask and if it is concerned that the agency might not call the person as a witness.

In either event, the testimony and assistance of managers and supervisors is crucial to the defense of the agency's decisions when they are challenged in an arbitration proceeding.

Your Role

By now you have probably concluded that contract administration is an important, on-going process and that supervisors and managers are essential to its success. If so, you are right. As a member of the management team, the decisions you make in the process of applying the labor agreement may directly affect the productivity and efficiency of your agency. Therefore, it is important to understand how to determine just what a contract means and how it should be applied in handling day-to-day situations in the workplace.

HOW ARBITRATORS READ AND APPLY LABOR AGREEMENTS

In carrying out your supervisory duties it is helpful if you understand how arbitrators look at and apply labor agreements. After all, if the union disagrees with the agency over what the contract means or how it should be applied, it may well be an arbitrator who makes the final decision.

First Things First

Arbitrators and others who are involved in labor relations work generally look at labor agreements as an outline of the rules and working conditions that union and management intended to create. When there is a grievance over what the contract means or how it should be applied in a particular situation, a good first step is to try to determine what the contract provision is intended to do. There are several steps you can take to help make this determination.

1. Read the contract to see if it has any provisions that apply to the specific situation at hand.

For example, if one of your employees is a union representative and you are unsure how much time she should be allowed to prepare a grievance for presentation, you might look at articles with titles like "Union Rights" or "Official Time" or "Grievance Procedure" to see if there is anything on the subject.

2. Pick the language that most directly applies to the situation.

For example, assume there are two provisions that seem to apply to the issue of official time. Assume that one, under "Union Rights," provides that representatives are entitled to a "reasonable amount of official time" for representational activities. The other, under "Grievance Procedure," says that representatives are entitled to a maximum of two hours at each step of the procedure to prepare grievances. Which would apply? The second, because it is most directly connected with the subject—the amount of time allowed to prepare grievances.

3. If the contract has language on the subject that is clear and can only be reasonably interpreted to mean one thing, that is how it should be applied.

For example, if a contract provision says that employees will be reimbursed only for the actual tuition cost of job-related courses, the rule is clear and usually will be applied just as it is written. In these situations arguments about past practices or other understandings usually do not have much impact. Therefore, a claim for payment of related expenses, such as parking fees, probably would fail.

4. If the contract language is *not* clear or if it says nothing directly about the problem you are trying to deal with, check with your labor relations specialist to see how such situations have been handled before. There may be an unwritten rule, usually called a "past practice," for dealing with the issue.

For example, if the contract provides that the "costs associated with off-duty, job-related courses will be reimbursed," it is not clear whether parking fees should be paid. In this situation it is helpful to look at how the parties have applied the language before (past practice), how previous claims or grievances were handled (previous decisions), and maybe even what the parties said about the provision when it was negotiated into the contract.

5. If none of those possibilities provide a clear answer—maybe this is the first time the question has come up—your agency may simply have to pick a reasonable position and explain it.

Sometimes in such situations the union and the agency pick different reasonable positions and stick to them, and often that is when the matter goes to arbitration. That's okay, because that is the purpose of the arbitration process. But in most cases, the contract can and should be applied without requiring outside help from an arbitrator.

What the Contract Includes

The discussion of how to go about figuring out the correct meaning and application of the contract should give you a pretty strong hint that the labor agreement really consists of something more than the words printed on its pages. Actually, the contract is like a snowball, with the printed words as the inner core of the snowball. Wrapped around the inner core are several additional layers of meaning that include:

★ The practices that show how the contract is actually applied

★ Grievance and arbitration decisions interpreting the contract

★ The statements negotiators made that explain the intended operation of a contract provision during contract negotiations.

Past Practices

An important concept that is often misunderstood in contract administration is that of *past practices*. First, what are past practices? Really nothing more than clearly established rules or ways of doing things that are agreed to by both sides, but not actually put into writing. In other words, a past practice is an unwritten rule or way of doing things. For a past practice to exist, there must be an established pattern of behavior that is:

1. Clear and consistent

2. Longstanding

3. Known and accepted by both parties.

For example, if you have allowed employees to take a 10 minute rest period at about mid-morning every day for the last several years, the parties have established an unwritten past practice. It is a clear and consistent pattern in behavior that has gone on for a long time with both sides knowing about it. In most cases, such a genuine past practice could not be changed without first informing and negotiating with the union.

A past practice is an unwritten rule or way of doing things.

Generally, if the "practice" is contrary to a controlling regulation, law, or clear contract provision, it is not considered binding. For example, if a manager had been allowing full time employees to work only a 20 hour workweek, there would not be a binding past practice because law and regulation require full-time employees to work 80 hours every two weeks. This "practice" could be stopped simply by notifying the employees that they will have to obey the controlling rules.

Similarly, if either party has a clear right to choose how to do something under the contract, the fact that it has followed a certain way of doing business for a long period of time does not mean that a practice has been established. For example, if the labor agreement gives management the right to determine shift starting and quitting times, the fact that the same hours have been worked for several years would not establish a binding past practice tying the activity to those hours. Management could still exercise its right to establish different starting and quitting times if it found it appropriate to do so. For similar reasons, the traditional assignment of three employees to a piece of equipment would not become a binding practice because management has the legal right to decide how many employees to assign to perform work. Therefore, it could decide to assign two employees to the job if it wanted to.

Determining Past Practices

The bottom line is that many things are called "past practices" that do not really measure up. Remember to look first at what the contract says. Then, if there is not a clear rule controlling the situation set down in the contract, check to see whether a claimed "past practice" is really consistent, longstanding, and accepted by both sides. Then, if the "practice" does not run afoul of a controlling regulation or management right, chances are that you have a genuine past practice.

A Very Important Rule

Sometimes you may come to the conclusion that a contract provision should be read and applied one way, but a union representative may reach a different conclusion. For example, if you direct an employee to work a weekend overtime assignment, the union may believe that you have improperly interpreted the contract and that someone else should have been given the assignment.

In such situations, a very important rule of contract administration applies. It is usually called the *work first, grieve later* rule. It means pretty much what it sounds like, and it works like this. In most situations, no matter how certain an employee or his representative may be that a manager or supervisor is applying the contract incorrectly, the employee does not have the right to disobey instructions. Rather, the employee must follow orders first and seek to fix the problem later—usually by filing a grievance.

NOTE: If an employee refuses to follow orders, even if he or she is ultimately found to have been correct in the interpretation of the contract, most arbitrators will still uphold discipline for insubordination because the employee does not have the right to disobey direct instructions.

The only clear exceptions to this rule are situations in which an employee refuses to follow instructions because a) he reasonably fears that obeying will place him in serious physical danger, or b) following the instruction would require him to commit an illegal or immoral act.

It is important to understand this rule and to advise employees of it in dealing with routine problems that might come up under the contract.

USING OFFICIAL TIME

A contract administration problem worthy of special mention is the use of official time by union representatives. "Official time" is the term used throughout the Federal Government to refer to the time used by a union representative to represent a union while still being paid by the agency.

The labor relations law states that a union representative is entitled to receive official time to engage in *representational activities* in any amount the agency and the union agree to be "reasonable, necessary, and in the public interest." The first question you may have is, "What are representational activities?" In general, they include efforts on behalf of bargaining unit employees, such as investigating or presenting grievances, meeting with managers, serving on joint safety committees and the like.

Although union officials are entitled to negotiate a collective bargaining agreement with the agency, you are most likely to be affected by requests for time to engage in other representational activities—such as handling an employee's grievance or discussing a problem with working conditions for unit employees.

What's Not Covered

A representative is *not* entitled to use official time to carry out *internal union* business. This generally includes such things as soliciting new members, working on a union newsletter, election of union representatives, or collection of dues.

Any internal union business must be conducted on the representative's own time, such as before or after work, while on annual leave, or during a lunch break.

Read Your Agreement

Granting or denying official time is a contract administration decision that should be handled just as you would any other labor relations situations. Therefore, the first step you should take is to carefully read the applicable contract language to see how it applies to a representative's request for time. In some cases, your contract will establish specific guidelines for granting or denying the amount of time that can be used. If that is the case, your job will be straightforward—you only need to determine whether the amount of time requested falls within the constraints in the agreement. In many agreements, however, you will find that the contract only says that a representative is entitled to "reasonable time."

In interpreting and applying "reasonable" you will want to check with your labor relations advisor to determine the past practice of your organization, whether any grievance or arbitration decisions have been issued on the subject in your organization, and whether there is any bargaining history that will shed some light on how to handle your specific problem. You should also become familiar with any internal management policy used in your agency on use of official time.

The keys to dealing with "reasonable time" provisions are:

- Be reasonable but firm in ruling on requests for time

- Be consistent in your decisions.

If there are no past practices and you are in the unique position of interpreting "reasonable" for the first time, remember that your decision will become the starting point for establishing a practice on this subject. So give it some thought rather than making a "spur-of-the-moment" decision.

Exercise Your Authority

Finally, remember that if you are the supervisor of a union representative, you should not give up your responsibility to manage your organization.You are responsible for deciding whether a representative should be allowed to leave the worksite, just as any other employee must obtain your permission to leave. The use of official time is not automatic—it can only be used with your permission. So, after checking with your labor relations advisor, decide how to handle this sensitive issue and then be consistent in your administration of it.

ROLE OF THE LABOR RELATIONS ADVISOR

The labor relations advisor plays a key role in helping you successfully administer the labor agreement. You should seek the advice of your labor relations staff for guidance on any agreements that may have been previously reached with the union. For example, there may be settlements in grievances that you may not be aware of that could directly impact the interpretation of a contract article. Or there may be an established approach to applying an unclear contract provision. Your labor relations staff will be aware of such things and will help you to deal with any problems that may come up.

Additionally, the labor relations office normally has notes from the previous bargaining sessions that can be helpful in determining the meaning of contract language. Without checking, you may not be aware of facts critical to your final decision in applying the agreement.

In short, your role in interpreting the agreement is a critical one. *The labor relations staff is there to help you, but they can only do so if you let them know what you are doing and what problems you are having.*

Key Points

1. Labor agreements consist of the words in the contract and also the practices, decisions and explanations of the parties. The union has an equal voice in how the contract should be interpreted and applied.

2. Supervisors and managers carry the primary management responsibility for interpreting, applying and enforcing the labor agreement. Regardless of how well your agency's bargaining team may have done in negotiating a contract, the agreement is only as good as the supervisors who apply it in real-life situations on the job.

3. The intent of the contract is found by looking first at the words of the agreement, then by looking to such things as past practices, previous grievance and arbitration decisions, and bargaining history.

4. Past practices are built on longstanding, consistent patterns of behavior that both parties know about and accept.

5. Employees are required to follow instructions first and, if they feel the orders are incorrect under the labor agreement, to file a grievance later. There are only a few exceptions to this rule, and failure to follow it can lead to discipline for insubordination.

6. Your agency's labor relations specialists are an essential resource in helping you to read and apply the labor agreement effectively.

Chapter
Five

Handling
Grievances

INTRODUCTION

In a popular movie from several years ago, the main character urged people to deal with things that made them angry or unhappy by throwing open a window, sticking their heads out, and yelling "I'm mad as hell and I'm not going to take it any more!" Although it may have looked odd to the neighbors, it was probably very satisfying, at least for the moment.

Unfortunately, that approach probably did not solve the problems that were getting under their skin. Luckily, the labor relations law provides a mechanism for employees, unions and agencies to work out their problems in a more effective way. This mechanism is the *negotiated grievance procedure*, and it must be included in every Federal sector labor agreement. It is important for you to understand what the grievance procedure is, how it works, and how to deal with the problems— grievances—that are raised through it.

THE GRIEVANCE PROCEDURE

Although your agency and the union representing your employees are free to design your own procedures for handling grievances, most grievance procedures fall into a basic pattern. Usually they are made up of several levels or "steps" at which a grievance can be presented to agency managers.

Structure

Most grievance procedures are built on 3 or 4 steps. Step 1 is usually the first level supervisor. In most grievance procedures, grievances may be informally filed at this level—that is, they can be filed orally and do not have to be into writing. At this level the supervisor is also usually allowed to answer orally rather than in writing.

In most cases, problems are effectively handled and resolved at this informal level. If the matter is not settled, however, several additional steps involving higher level managers are usually available. The next steps involve not only higher levels of agency management, but are also more formal. In most cases, grievances must be presented and answered in writing at these levels.

The final step of the grievance procedure, as required by law, is *arbitration*. This means that either the union or management may place an unresolved grievance before a neutral person, called an *arbitrator*, to decide the issue. Arbitration works like a "People's Court," complete with a "rent-a-judge," as a final way to deal with problems that come up under the labor agreement. Once appointed, the arbitrator has the power to issue a final, binding and enforceable decision on the grievance.

Time Limits

Contracts usually set up time limits for the filing of grievances, both at the first step and from one level to the next. Failure to file or pursue a grievance within the stated time limits often results in a claim that the grievance is "untimely." Grievances may be dismissed on that basis.

Also, there are usually time limits for a supervisor to answer a grievance. If an answer is not delivered within the stated time limit, contracts frequently allow the union or grieving employee to move the grievance to the next step without waiting any longer for an answer. In a few contracts, failure to answer within the established time limits may result in the grievance being automatically granted. *So be careful to keep an eye on the time limits set up in the grievance procedure.*

Typical Steps in a Negotiated Grievance Procedure

1. First line supervisor

2. Manager

3. Director

4. Arbitration

Purpose of the Negotiated Grievance Procedure

The law requires that every Federal sector labor agreement must contain a grievance procedure, so it is apparent it is there to serve an important purpose. Actually, it serves several important purposes.

1. Communication Channel

The grievance procedure provides an acceptable way for employees and union representatives to raise questions about how a rule or working condition is applied. Although sometimes annoying, grievances are vastly preferable to slow-downs, sick leave abuse or outright hostility in the workplace.

2. Development Device

It is through the processing and resolution of grievances that the contract develops much of its meaning. For example, a grievance decision that an assignment to openings on another shift shall be offered to qualified employees in seniority order might clarify and develop the meaning of a provision on seniority.

3. Enforcement Mechanism

If the union, an employee or even management believe that the other side is not living up to the rules established in the labor agreement, the contract provisions can be enforced by filing a grievance. In practice, of course, most grievances are filed by unions or employees protesting decisions made by managers and supervisors.

What Is A Grievance?

What is a grievance? A good place to start defining a grievance is by looking at what the law says. The labor relations statute gives a broad definition providing that a grievance is "any complaint" by an agency, a labor organization (union) or an employee about "any matter relating to the employment of the employee" or the "interpretation or claim of breach" of a labor agreement or the "violation, misinterpretation or misapplication of any law, rule or regulation affecting the conditions of employment."

What's Covered

In plain English that boils down to meaning that a unit employee or union representative can file a grievance under the negotiated grievance procedure about almost anything that is associated with employees' conditions of employment. Those, you should remember, include personnel policies, practices and general working conditions. In most cases the grievance would be based on a claim that some action—or inaction—by agency management violates either a rule, regulation or practice contained in the contract or elsewhere, such as agency personnel regulations.

For example, if an employee felt that she was improperly required to obtain a doctor's certificate in violation of the procedure set up in the labor agreement, a grievance could be filed. Similarly, if an employee felt that the agency violated its merit promotion plan in not advertising a vacancy for the minimum time required in the regulation, she could also grieve that matter, even though it is not written directly into the contract. Another common kind of grievance might challenge a disciplinary action taken against a unit employee.

What's Not Covered

The law sets aside a few specific issues that *cannot* be dealt with through the grievance procedure. These include disputes over prohibited political activities; retirement, life and health insurance matters; suspensions or removals for national security; examination, certification or appointment matters; and any classification matter that does not result in a reduction in grade or pay. In other words, not many subjects are taken out of the reach of the grievance procedure by the law itself. Subjects that cannot be grieved under the contract are usually called "non-grievable" matters.

The parties are also free to negotiate over what things will or will not be included in the coverage of the grievance procedure (usually called the "scope" of the procedure). Sometimes they agree that other issues will not be "grievable" under the contract procedure. For example, some contracts specify that the failure to adopt a suggestion is not grievable. Others provide that the termination of a detail cannot be grieved. So it is important to become familiar with the scope or coverage of the grievance procedure in your particular contract. You can do that by carefully reading the first few sections of the "Negotiated Grievance Procedure" article, where the coverage is usually spelled out.

Participants in the Grievance Process

A number of participants are usually involved in handling and resolving a grievance. Let's look at these participants and the roles they play in order to fully understand how you fit into this process.

The Grievant

First, of course, is a grievant. In order to present a convincing case for the granting of a remedy, it must usually be demonstrated that the grievant (the person filing the grievance) has been damaged in some way.

Who may file and process grievances under a labor agreement? First, individual *unit employees* or a group of unit employees may file a grievance contending that the contract has been violated. For example, a group of employees might file a grievance seeking payment of environmental differential or hazard pay.

Employees may file grievances on their own behalf and present them to management without the assistance or concurrence of a union representative. But they are *not* allowed to use any representative other than the union. (That is what is meant by the union's status as the exclusive representative of employees.)

Second, the *union* may file a grievance, either on its own behalf or for one or more unit employees. For example, a grievance on behalf of the union might address a reduction of official time granted to union officers. A grievance protesting the failure to grant a particular employee a temporary promotion while on detail might be filed on behalf of all employees who may be detailed.

Third, *management* may file a grievance against the union. In practice, this is rarely done as management normally makes the decisions and the union normally challenges decisions through the grievance procedure. On occasion, however, it is done. For example, if a union refused to pay its half of the cost for printing a labor agreement after agreeing to do so, an agency could file a grievance seeking payment of the bill.

The Union

The second participant in the grievance process is the union. Although some aspects of the union's role were discussed above, several other points regarding the union's role need to be considered.

First, recognize that one of the union's primary functions is to represent grievants diligently, competently, and even aggressively if the situation demands it. Union representatives are within their rights to request information that is relevant and necessary to the investigation of a grievance, or potential grievance; to disagree with management officials' opinions and approaches to issues; and to present the grievant's case in clear and forceful terms.

Since grievances are usually a challenge to a decision or action by a management official, forceful representation may present an unusual and difficult situation for managers to handle.

It is important for you to remember that when a union representative is representing employees or the union in grievances, he or she is engaging in a *protected activity* under the labor relations statute. In practical terms, this means that union officials are entitled to deal with management officials on an *equal footing* while carrying out such functions. Words and behavior that might be unacceptable in a supervisor-subordinate context are often considered proper and routine while handling a grievance. This does not mean that union officials are able to indulge in unnecessarily disrespectful or offensive behavior just because they are representing a grievant. But it does mean they have greater room to disagree with you than they do when in their role as subordinate employees.

Questions concerning the allowable limits of such behavior must, of course, be determined on a case-by-case basis. Questions in this area should be referred to your agency's labor relations experts.

The Role of Supervisors and Managers

The role of the individual supervisor or manager in grievance processing is the most crucial one. The grievant and the union only have to claim that certain facts exist, to contend that the asserted facts add up to a violation of the labor contract, and to specify the remedy they feel is appropriate. The management official responding to a grievance faces a far more difficult task. If you doubt this, consider the following list of things you must do when handling a grievance.

1. Receive the grievance

This involves several important functions. First, it means that you are responsible for obtaining a reasonably complete, accurate picture of the facts asserted by the grievant as well as the union's or grievant's theory on why the claimed facts—if correct—violate the contract. You are also required to assure that all requirements are met in receiving the grievance. This means, for example, that meetings must be held with the grievant within specified time limits, and that the union must be given an opportunity to attend the meeting.

Similarly, you are responsible for making certain that the grievance is filed in line with the contract's procedural requirements. For example, you should check to make sure that the grievance was filed within the time limits specified in the agreement and that it has been referred to the proper levels of management as required by the contract. In short, it is your job to make sure the rules are followed.

2. Investigate the grievance

As a management official you bear primary responsibility for determining whether the facts given by the grievant are accurate and complete, or whether additional information is needed. This may require you to meet with other employees and managers to get a clear picture of the facts surrounding the grievance, and to pull together documents or other evidence that will help you in reaching a sound decision.

This also means that when there are more than one version of the facts, you must use your judgment to decide what is fact and what is fancy.

In addition, you are responsible for reviewing the provisions of the labor agreement and any existing practices related to the issue, and for determining how they may have been applied in similar situations in the past.

3. Respond to the grievance

Management officials are also responsible for developing and delivering grievance responses that are procedurally and substantively correct. What does this mean? First, it means that you must review the matter within the time limits specified in the contract, and that the grievance response must meet any other procedural requirements contained in the agreement. Second, it means that sometimes you must sift through conflicting claims and different versions of an incident to develop an accurate version of what has happened. Third, you must then figure out the intended meaning of contract provisions and fairly apply them to the situation at hand.

Finally, you must deliver a fair and correct decision. Your decision will become part of the record of the grievance, and it will be important later, particularly if the matter goes to arbitration.

These are the reasons we say that managers and supervisors have the most difficult and important role in processing grievances.

Practical Advice

There are three things you should note in connection with the right of employees to file a grievance:

1. Allow Union Representation in Meetings

Even if an employee is presenting a grievance without using the union as his or her representative, the union is still entitled to be present during meetings held with the employee to discuss the grievance. The union has this right because, as you may recall from Chapter Three, grievance meetings are considered *formal discussions* under the labor relations statute.

2. Apply the Contract

The way you resolve a grievance must be consistent with the collective bargaining agreement and existing personnel policies and practices. For example, it would not be correct to resolve an employee's grievance on overtime by providing the employee with a remedy that conflicts with overtime distribution procedures in the agreement. This approach would probably just lead to a ULP charge and/or another grievance from the union.

3. Don't Take It Personally

Although we commonly speak and think in terms of grievances being "filed against" a supervisor or manager, the grievance system is not designed to attack or punish any individual. A grievance is filed to correct a real or perceived problem and should be viewed that way. Therefore, the best thing to do is to stay calm, not view the grievance as a personal insult, and attempt to give the best answer possible.

A Final Word on Grievance Handling

A brief glance at these requirements will, we hope, convince you that even in relatively simple cases, grievance handling is not as easy as falling off the proverbial log—at least not if you want to do it well. In some situations, it can be particularly difficult to handle well. For example, if you are the second or third step in the grievance procedure, often you will be required to respond to appeals of decisions already rendered by subordinate supervisors or managers. In these situations, it is easy to adopt one of several ill-advised approaches to the process.

Rubberstamping

★ If your subordinates have already issued a decision, don't bother to determine whether the facts and logic are well developed. It is safe to assume they have done a good job. After all, you picked them!

Solidarity

★ Maintain a united front when dealing with employees and unions! Stick together regardless of whether the decision makes sense!

<u>Sandbagging</u>

★ While your subordinate's decision was well written and sound, grant additional relief to the grievant anyway. This let's everyone in your agency know who really has the power to make things happen!

Don't fall into these traps. Remember, the best, simplest and smartest thing to do is to handle each grievance like a professional umpire: Call every one exactly as you see it.

Key Points

1. The negotiated grievance procedure serves a variety of important functions for management as well as employees.

2. The scope (coverage) of the grievance procedure is determined through the collective bargaining process. In general, almost all employee complaints can be raised through the negotiated grievance procedure.

3. In preparing and presenting grievances, union officials have equal status with the management officials with whom they are dealing.

4. Supervisors and managers bear primary responsibility for receiving, investigating, and responding to grievances.

5. The best approach to handling grievances is to deal with each one on its individual merits. Rubber-stamping or sandbagging subordinate management officials' decisions will only decrease morale and increase organizational problems.

Chapter Six

Unfair
Labor
Practices

INTRODUCTION

In the first chapter, you learned of a number of important rights guaranteed to employees, unions and management. But what guarantees that these rights will be applied correctly? If a law has no teeth it has little meaning.

The Federal labor relations law allows employees, unions, and agencies to complain of a violation of the law and to get relief if a violation has occurred. Violations of this particular law are called unfair labor practices. If an unfair labor practice (ULP) is found, a remedy can and will be ordered.

In practice, most unfair labor practices are filed by unions against agencies. The reason for this is simple. Agency management has the authority to take—or not take—action in managing the organization. If the union or employees believe an agency's actions are improper, one way to deal with them is through the unfair labor practice process. Management is rarely in the position of challenging a union action, since unions do not make operational decisions. Therefore, agencies rarely file ULP's.

Because actions of supervisors and managers are most often challenged through the filing of ULP's, and because supervisors often become directly involved in the processing of ULP issues, it is important that you understand how this process works and where you fit in it.

THE ULP PROCESS

Unions and employees file thousands of ULP's every year. But what happens when a union decides to file an unfair labor practice about something going on in your part of the organization? Who is the charge against? Who is responsible? How will the charge be handled, and what, if anything, should you do? Probably the best way to answer these and other practical questions is by starting with an explanation of what happens when a ULP charge is filed.

Charge

If a union believes that you or other managers have taken an action that violates a right provided by the law—for example, that you have changed a personnel policy or working condition without first notifying and bargaining with the union—it may file an unfair labor practice charge with the Federal Labor Relations Authority. The FLRA has several regional offices, and the charge normally would be filed with the office that covers your region of the country.

ULP charges must be filed on a standard form supplied by the FLRA. Although you may be the management official directly involved and actually named in the charge form, the ULP charge is against *the agency*, not you as an individual.

Investigation

Upon receiving a charge form, the FLRA region puts a case number on it and assigns it to an agent for investigation. A copy of the charge is also sent to the agency for its information. After allowing a fifteen day delay to give the parties an opportunity to settle the problem informally, an FLRA agent will begin an investigation. This usually involves meeting with the person who filed the charge as well as others who may have knowledge of the matter—including managers and supervisors who may be named in the charge or otherwise involved.

As part of the investigation the Authority agent can be expected to take careful notes, to collect documents or other evidence that may be important, and to ask for a written, sworn statement—usually called an affidavit—from witnesses interviewed in connection with the charge. Such investigations are usually conducted "on the clock" without any charge to leave.

> **NOTE: You are entitled to representation at any interview with an FLRA agent, and most agencies insist that supervisors and managers be accompanied by a labor relations specialist or an attorney at such meetings. The statements you make in this interview may later be used against your agency in prosecuting the unfair labor practice.**

In addition, some agencies advise supervisors and managers not to complete or sign written statements during or after such interviews. Be sure to check with your agency's labor relations practitioners to find out your agency's policy.

Settlement Efforts

During or shortly after the investigation, the FLRA agent may suggest one or more informal settlement possibilities as a way of resolving the issue. As a result, a substantial number of charges are informally worked out and resolved this way.

In cases in which it seems clear that there is no basis for finding a violation of the law, the FLRA agent may suggest that the union withdraw a charge. In such cases, if the union does not withdraw it, the FLRA regional office will consider the information it has developed through its investigation and decide whether it believes the matter should be taken further. If not, it will then dismiss the charge outright.

Complaint and Hearing

On the other hand, if the FLRA concludes that a ULP charge has merit—that is, it believes that a violation of the law can be proved—it will issue a formal complaint. This requires the agency either to settle the matter or to defend itself in a formal hearing before an Administrative Law Judge. The union's case is presented by an attorney from the General Counsel's office of the FLRA. The union is not required to provide its own legal representation. The agency, on the other hand, must provide its own defense—usually presented by agency attorneys or labor relations practitioners. They will normally require testimony by operating managers and supervisors to help present the agency's case.

If the issue is not resolved, the FLRA will arrange a hearing date and will present evidence in an effort to prove that the agency violated the law. The evidence may include your testimony about the situation involved in the charge. The time required by FLRA representatives to prepare for employees' testimony at hearing, as well as the time spent for actual attendance at it, is also on paid time without charge to leave.

Decision

Following the ULP hearing, if the matter goes that far, the Administrative Law Judge issues a recommended decision that may or may not find that an unfair labor practice has occurred. If neither side files an exception (appeal), the recommended decision becomes final. If either side does choose to appeal—which is usually the case—the matter goes to the full FLRA for a final decision.

Remedy

If the Authority decides that a ULP has been committed, it will order that certain remedial actions be taken. These can include several possible steps.

1. Cease and Desist Order and Posting

When a violation of the law is found the Authority will order that the agency post a notice ordering it to "cease and desist" (stop) the activity that is in violation of the law. Such notices must be signed by the head of the agency or field activity, and are posted for 60 days in all places where notices to employees are normally posted. This remedy is the minimum that can be ordered, and it is *always* directed when a violation is found. Depending on the violation, other steps may also be ordered.

2. Status Quo Ante Order

In cases where the Authority finds that an agency made an improper change without bargaining with the union, it often orders the agency to return to the *status quo*; that is, to the way things were before the improper change. This can involve replacing regulations or personnel policies, re-running personnel actions, reassigning or moving employees, or whatever else is necessary to put things back to the way they were before the improper change.

3. Make Whole Order

Where an agency's improper actions may have caused employees to lose pay, benefits, or differentials, the FLRA can issue a *make whole* order. Depending upon the agency's actions, this might include restoration of an employee to a position, a retroactive promotion, back pay for improperly denied overtime or other differentials, and in some cases, even attorney fees for the work performed by union attorneys in helping to present the ULP case.

4. Bargaining Order

In situations in which an agency improperly refuses to bargain with the union, the Authority can also order it to negotiate in good faith on the matters or proposals involved.

> **NOTE: Because ULP's are filed against agencies, not individual supervisors, there are no remedies directed at the manager or supervisor involved even if a violation of the law is found. The FLRA does not, for example, call for the discipline or removal of a supervisor based on a ULP finding.**

Most Common ULP's Committed by Management

Failure To Bargain

The overwhelming majority of ULP charges against management allege a failure to bargain with a union concerning conditions of employment for bargaining unit employees. How could an agency miss so many opportunities to negotiate? Unfortunately, it is easy to do. The most common situations in which agency officials run afoul of the bargaining obligation are listed below.

1. In carrying out an operational decision or in developing a new personnel policy or procedure, agency management implements its plans without first notifying the union soon enough to allow it a

reasonable opportunity to determine whether it wishes to request to bargain.

For example, a manager might decide to place a more stringent limit on the time allowed for employees to recuperate after donating blood, and publicizes the new rule without telling the union first. The failure to notify the union before changing a personnel policy constitutes a failure to bargain under the FLRA's interpretation of the labor relations statute.

2. In developing a new or different work procedure affecting unit employees' working conditions, management implements it without informing the union and affording it an opportunity to bargain on the impact and method of implementing the new procedure.

For example, in order to increase productivity, a supervisor might decide that employees should report directly to field locations rather than to a central office location, and implements the new method without first notifying the union. The change could affect a number of working conditions; for example, employees' transportation arrangements. Therefore, the union may wish to make proposals designed to soften the adverse impact of the change. Again, failure to notify the union may form a valid basis for finding that the agency has committed a ULP.

3. Agency management informs the union of an intended change such as those outlined above, but refuses to bargain on the union's proposals because, in management's opinion, the action it intends to

take involves a management right guaranteed by the statute. For example, a manager decides that the workload could best be handled by creating an additional shift. When he informs the union of his intention to create a new shift, he refuses to bargain with the union over proposals on how to pick employees for assignment to the new shift.

4. Agency management concludes that a provision in the labor agreement or a well established past practice is no longer appropriate or convenient and changes it. For example, a supervisor may decide that a contract provision requiring him to ask for volunteers before assigning overtime is more trouble than it is worth, and no longer asks for volunteers. This direct, deliberate breach of an established condition of employment is considered a rejection of the negotiated contract and, therefore, a refusal to bargain in good faith with the union.

Other Common ULP Charges

Other fairly common ULP charges focus on the failure or refusal of management officials to allow union representatives to attend or participate in Weingarten and formal discussion meetings; refusal to provide information necessary for the union to investigate or process a grievance or to bargain on behalf of unit employees; and assertions that agency management has discriminated against employees in taking various personnel actions (for example, promotions or discipline) based on their union involvement.

Nevertheless, ULP charges alleging an improper failure or refusal to bargain make up the great majority of unfair labor practice charges against agency management.

Fortunately, it is easy to avoid most such disputes by following a few simple steps. Applying this approach is known as "practicing ULP avoidance" and requires only a minor investment in management training. Ignoring this approach is comparable to putting on blinders and hoping for the best. Following this "head in the sand" approach, on the other hand, usually requires a substantial investment in time spent talking to FLRA agents, attorneys, labor relations specialists, and Administrative Law Judges—at the agency's expense.

Avoiding ULP's

Unfortunately, avoiding ULP charges is not a matter that is completely within the control of agency management. After all, employees and unions are free to file a charge whenever they want. There is no standard of quality or likely merit that charges must meet before being investigated by the FLRA.

And, in fact, a large percentage of ULP charges filed by unions or employees are found not to have any merit, either because the facts are inaccurate or because the facts do not constitute a ULP even if true.

Nevertheless, although an agency cannot completely prevent the filing of ULP charges, it *is* within an agency's power to minimize the number of valid charges that are filed. Also, an agency can take steps to help reduce the number of charges that do not have any merit. First let's look at the steps that can be taken to hold down the number of valid charges:

The first and most important step in ULP avoidance is the one you have already taken in reading this book: Becoming knowledgeable of your responsibilities under the Federal labor-management relations program and, if possible, receiving training in how to meet these responsibilities.

Second, since the overwhelming majority of ULP charges involve "failure to bargain" issues, you should be careful to determine whether intended changes affect unit employees, and, if so, inform and deal with their union.

Third, communicate with *the union,* rather than directly with employees. Ensure that you do not hold "formal discussions" without allowing the union an opportunity to be represented. Also, make certain that the union is allowed to represent employees during investigative discussions that could lead to disciplinary action if requested by an employee.

Fourth, make certain that your personnel-related decisions are not be based on an employee's involvement in union activities. Bear in mind that it is often as important to avoid the appearance that personnel decisions are based on an employee's union activities as it is to avoid actually making decisions based on these considerations.

Finally, help to reduce the time and effort required to respond to ULP charges by adopting an aggressive posture in reacting to them. This requires you to respond quickly and directly to those who file the charges, determine the source and dimensions of the problem, clear up possible misconceptions, and communicate with the employees or union officials making the charges. This approach often results in a faster and more satisfactory settlement of charges than sitting back and waiting to see who wins.

ROLE OF YOUR LABOR RELATIONS EXPERTS

Your labor relations representatives should be consulted promptly whenever a ULP is filed or you think one is going to be filed. Often a lot of time and money can be saved if the problem is handled early in the process. Once a charge is filed, resolution is more difficult and more complicated.

As a supervisor, you are not expected to be knowledgeable of all the fine points of labor relations case law. Your labor relations representative will help you to analyze the situation you are facing and will be able to explore alternatives and possible ways to resolve the problem with you.

Trying to resolve the problem without using your agency's experts is unnecessary and unwise. The resource is there so use it to your own advantage!

Key Points

1. Violation of a party's rights under the Federal labor-management relations statute is an unfair labor practice. Such violations can result from taking a prohibited action or from failing to carry out an action required by the law.

2. A right granted by the labor relations statute is enforced through the ULP process. A ULP violation may be remedied through a variety of means, including "cease and desist" orders, awards of back pay, and other steps.

3. Most ULP charges are filed by unions or employees complaining of an action by a management official. Most charges allege a failure to bargain as required by the statute.

4. Supervisors and managers play the central role in avoiding, responding to, and resolving ULP's.

5. Most meritorious ULP charges can be avoided by training supervisors and managers in their rights and responsibilities under the statute.

6. Agencies follow different approaches in responding to ULP charges and investigations. Consequently, management officials should talk with labor relations officials before responding to the FLRA.

7. An active, aggressive response to ULP charges will frequently save time and money by disposing of most problems promptly and by improving communications with unions and employees.

Other FPMi Publications Available

To order additional copies of *The Supervisor's Guide to Federal Labor Relations* or any of the other publications from FPMi, Inc., call or send your order to:

Federal Personnel Management Institute, Inc.
3322 South Memorial Parkway
Suite 40
Huntsville, AL 35801
(205) 882-3042

FPMi publications include:

The Supervisor's Guide to Federal Labor Relations ($6.95)

The Federal Manager's Guide to Discipline ($6.95)

The Federal Manager's Guide to Preventing Sexual Harassment ($5.95)

The Federal Supervisor's Guide to Drug Testing ($5.95)

The Federal Employee's Guide to Drug Testing ($2.75)

The Federal Manager's Guide to EEO ($7.95)

Performance Standards Made Simple!: A Practical Guide for Federal Managers and Supervisors ($6.95)

Grievance Arbitration in the Federal Service ($35.00)

The Bargaining Book: A Guide to Collective Bargaining in the Federal Government ($9.95)

The Union Representative's Guide to Federal Labor Relations ($8.95)

The Federal Labor & Employee Relations Update ($125.00) (The *Update* is a monthly publication. The price is for a one year subscription.)

Please call for information on quantity discounts.

FPMi Training Seminars for Federal Supervisors and Managers

The Federal Personnel Management Institute, Inc. specializes in training seminars for *Federal* managers and supervisors. These seminars can usually be conducted at your worksite at a per person rate that is substantially less than open enrollment seminars.

Each seminar includes a copy of the appropriate book for each participant as well as a workbook including copies of all workshops and materials presented in the seminar.

The instructors for FPMi seminars have all had practical experience with the Federal Government and know problems Federal supervisors face and how to deal effectively with those problems.

Some of the seminar-workshops available include:

"Managing Unionized Employees Effectively"

"Basic Labor Relations Workshop"

"Managing Labor Relations Conflict"

"Negotiating a Federal Labor Agreement"

"The Federal Drug Testing Program"

"How to Take Effective Disciplinary Action"

"How to Write Effective Performance Standards"

For more Information contact FPMi at:

Federal Personnel Management Institute, Inc.
3322 South Memorial Parkway
Suite 40
Huntsville, AL 35801
(205) 882-3042